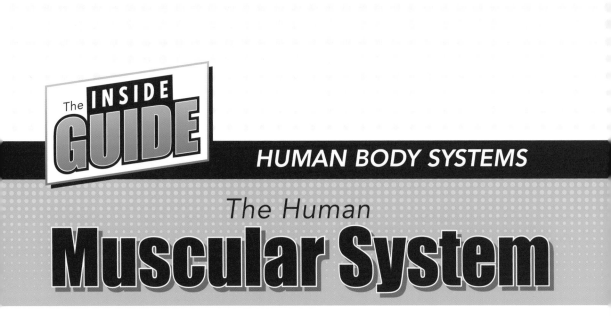

The INSIDE GUIDE

HUMAN BODY SYSTEMS

The Human
Muscular System

By Cassie M. Lawton

Cavendish Square

New York

Published in 2021 by Cavendish Square Publishing, LLC
243 5th Avenue, Suite 136, New York, NY 10016

Copyright © 2021 by Cavendish Square Publishing, LLC

First Edition

Website: cavendishsq.com

This publication represents the opinions and views of the author based on his or her personal experience, knowledge, and research. The information in this book serves as a general guide only. The author and publisher have used their best efforts in preparing this book and disclaim liability rising directly or indirectly from the use and application of this book.

Portions of this work were originally authored by Greg Roza and published as *The Muscular System (The Human Body)*. All new material this edition authored by Cassie M. Lawton.

All websites were available and accurate when this book was sent to press.

Cataloging-in-Publication Data

Names: Lawton, Cassie M.
Title: The human muscular system / Cassie M. Lawton.
Description: First edition. | New York : Cavendish Square, 2021. | Series: The inside guide: human body systems | Includes glossary and index.
Identifiers: ISBN 9781502657251 (pbk.) | ISBN 9781502657275 (library bound) | ISBN 9781502657268 (6 pack) | ISBN 9781502657282 (ebook)
Subjects: LCSH: Musculoskeletal system–Juvenile literature.
Classification: LCC QM151.L39 2021 | DDC 612.7–dc23

Editor: Kristen Susienka
Copy Editor: Nathan Heidelberger
Designer: Deanna Paternostro

The photographs in this book are used by permission and through the courtesy of: Cover S K Chavan/Shutterstock.com; p. 4 Microgen/Shutterstock.com; p. 6 michaeljung/Shutterstock.com; pp. 7, 12 BlueRingMedia/Shutterstock.com; p. 8 Sebastian Kaulitzki/Shutterstock.com; p. 9 (right, left) design36/Shutterstock.com; p. 10 Liya Graphics/Shutterstock.com; p. 13 Designua/Shutterstock.com; p. 14 Vecton/Shutterstock.com; p. 15 Alex Mit/Shutterstock.com; p. 16 lzf/Shutterstock.com; p. 18 Billion Photos/Shutterstock.com; p. 19 Magic mine/Shutterstock.com; p. 20 Aleksandar Karanov/Shutterstock.com; p. 21 Twinsterphoto/Shutterstock.com; p. 22 nikolaborovic/Shutterstock.com; p. 23 Andrey_Popov/Shutterstock.com; p. 24 (top) Leszek Glasner/Shutterstock.com; p. 24 (bottom) ChiccoDodiFC/Shutterstock.com; p. 25 Africa Studio/Shutterstock.com; p. 27 Rasulov/Shutterstock.com; p. 28 (top) Syda Productions/Shutterstock.com; p. 28 (bottom) Monkey Business Images/Shutterstock.com; p. 29 (top) Sion Touhig/Getty Images News/Getty Images; p. 29 (bottom) Maridav/Shutterstock.com.

Some of the images in this book illustrate individuals who are models. The depictions do not imply actual situations or events.

CPSIA compliance information: Batch #CS20CSQ: For further information contact Cavendish Square Publishing LLC, New York, New York, at 1-877-980-4450.

Printed in the United States of America

Find us on

CONTENTS

Humans have hundreds of muscles that help them move.

THE MAGIC OF MUSCLES

The human body has many different parts that work together to make it function. Muscles are an important part of the human body, and there are a lot of them! In fact, there are around 650 skeletal muscles in the human body—and they all help us move in different ways. They're part of the muscular system, or the system in the human body that deals with muscle movements. Without them, we wouldn't be able to move at all!

Think of all the ways the muscles in your body move in a normal day. Your hand muscles help you turn doorknobs and hold pens. Your arm muscles help you lift phones and throw balls. Your leg muscles help you kick, jump, and run. Even the muscles in your face allow you to show emotion.

There's much more to our muscles than you might imagine. Some muscles, such as the kind found in the heart, work without us even thinking about them. Some help us swallow food or go to the bathroom.

Fast Fact

Where muscles meet bones, they taper down to tough yet flexible cords called tendons. Tendons transfer motion from muscles to bones. They grow into the bones to form a strong connection that's very hard to break.

BUILDING UP THE BODY'S MUSCLES

There are many ways to make the body's muscles stronger. Sometimes, people enjoy making their muscles very big—so big, in fact, that they often look like giants! People who do this are called bodybuilders. Bodybuilders increase the size of their muscles by lifting weights regularly at the gym and eating a special diet. Lifting weights actually damages the cells of the muscles. However, the muscles grow larger and stronger as they heal, especially if the person eats the right types of foods. Protein is a **nutrient** found in many foods that helps repair damaged muscle cells. Bodybuilders use this to their advantage, but so can regular people. By eating foods that are high in protein, such as meat, fish, and nuts, you can make sure your muscles stay healthy.

Bodybuilders work hard to make their muscles bigger.

Before we look at those other, special types of muscles, let's take a look at the most common type of muscle found in the human body: skeletal muscles.

The Skeleton's Muscles

Skeletal muscles are the muscles attached to bones. They're **complex** body parts made up of bundles of long, **cylindrical** parts called fascicles. The fascicles are bundled together inside a covering called the epimysium. A single fascicle contains numerous muscle cells, which are called fibers. Between all fascicles are connective tissues that hold the cylindrical tissues in place. Blood vessels and nerves run through these connective tissues.

Muscle fibers themselves contain bundles of small, cylindrical proteins called myofibrils. Inside the myofibrils are thick and thin **filaments**, called myofilaments, that can slide past each other. This sliding action allows muscles to contract, or grow shorter.

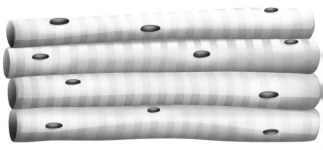

This illustration is an example of what skeletal muscle looks like.

Skeletal muscles are also called striated muscles. This is because they have light and dark striations, or stripes, that can be seen under a microscope.

Voluntary Movers

Unlike the other kinds of muscles, skeletal muscles are moved voluntarily. This means we have to think about moving them. When you want to move your body, electrical impulses travel from your brain,

Highlighted here is the Achilles tendon. It runs from the middle of your leg to your heel.

down your spinal column, through your nerves, and to the cells of your skeletal muscles.

Between the nerve cells and muscle cells is a very tiny gap. The electrical impulses tell the nerve cells to release special chemicals that cross the gap and enter the muscle cells. The chemicals tell the myofilaments inside the muscle cells to slide past each other. The cells—which are normally long and cylindrical—become shorter and fatter. This action tightens the muscle and creates movement, which is transferred along the tendons to the bones.

Twitch and Tetanus

Muscle cells are either "off" (relaxed) or "on" (contracted). However, the amount of time the cell remains contracted varies. A quick, single contraction is called a twitch. A twitch occurs, for example, when you blink your eye, which takes a fraction of a second. When a series of twitches occur one after another, the muscle cells remain contracted for a longer period of time. This sustained contraction is called tetanus. Tetanus is also the name of an illness caused by a kind of bacteria—very tiny living things. It causes the muscles to contract uncontrollably.

Up Close

Examples are helpful when learning about muscles. Let's take a look at the muscles of the upper arm. On the back of your arm is an extensor muscle called the triceps. When this muscle contracts, it causes your arm to extend at the elbow and straighten out. Once your arm is extended, the triceps muscle relaxes. A muscle called the biceps is on the front of your arm. This muscle is a flexor. When the biceps muscle contracts, your elbow flexes, or bends. Once your elbow is bent, the biceps relaxes.

Muscles called abductors and adductors work together the same way the extensors and flexors do. Imagine a straight line running from the top of your head to the floor between your feet. Any muscle that moves a body part away from that line is an abductor, such as the deltoid muscles of your shoulders. Any muscle that moves a body part toward the line is an adductor, such as the "lats," which are the largest muscles of your back.

The body's muscles are complex, and they're all important!

Abductors (*left*) and adductors (*right*) help move body parts such as your arms and back.

The heart is made up of a certain kind of muscle called cardiac muscle.

MAJOR MUSCLES

The muscles work in different ways to help the body. Some muscles work without us trying, while others only work when we think about them. Some of the most important muscles in the body work without us really thinking about it. If they stopped working, we'd be in trouble!

Cardiac Muscle

The heart is one of the most important muscles in the body. It's made mostly of special heart-specific, or cardiac, muscle. This kind of muscle makes up the largest layer of the heart walls, known as the myocardium. Like skeletal muscle, cardiac muscle is striated, or striped. The heart also moves by contracting. The actions that cause cardiac muscle cells to contract are nearly the same as those in skeletal muscle cells. However, cardiac muscle fibers are much shorter. They branch out and connect together in a complex network.

Cardiac muscle moves involuntarily. That means we don't have to think about moving cardiac muscle to keep our heart beating. Individual cardiac muscle cells aren't told to contract by electrical impulses from the brain. The electrical signals are generated, or

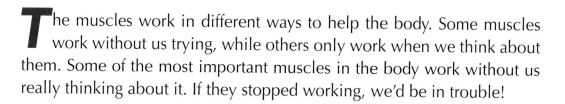

Fast Fact

The term "myocardium" comes from the Greek words for "muscle" and "heart."

created, within the myocardium itself. Special cardiac cells—called pacemaker cells—use chemical reactions to start the signals, which then travel from cell to cell throughout the heart. The amount of times a cardiac muscle can contract and relax in one's lifetime might surprise you: more than 2 billion times! That's a lot of hard work for one muscle.

Meeting of Cardiac Muscles

The meeting point between cardiac muscle cells is called an intercalated disk. These membranes have two functions. First, they help bind cells to each other. Second, they allow the cells to communicate with each other. Similar to the way nerve cells communicate with skeletal muscle cells, one cardiac muscle cell releases chemicals into an intercalated disk. The next cell receives the chemicals and passes the information along as an electrical impulse.

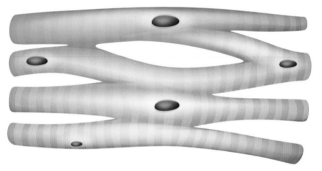

Shown here is a closer look at cardiac muscle.

Smooth Muscle

Smooth muscle is another kind of involuntary muscle. It forms the inner surfaces of many hollow organs. When viewed under a microscope, smooth muscle doesn't have striations. This is where its name comes from.

Smooth muscle cells are much smaller than skeletal muscle cells. They're wide in the middle and tapered on the ends. Many cells fit tightly together to form thin sheets. The sheets lie one on top of another to form thick layers of muscle.

Just like the other two types of muscle cells, smooth muscle cells contain bundles of thick and thin filaments that move past each other to contract. However, smooth muscle cells also have additional filaments that crisscross the cell and hold the bundles together. When

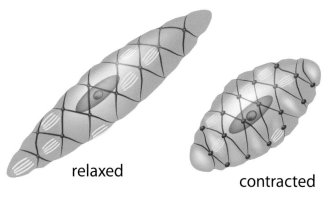

relaxed

contracted

Shown here is what a smooth muscle cell looks like when it's relaxed and contracted.

a smooth muscle cell contracts, the additional filaments tighten and squeeze the cell together like the drawstring on the opening of a purse or backpack.

Smooth muscle helps the body carry out numerous functions necessary for life without us even thinking about them. Most smooth muscle helps in the carrying of nutrients, chemicals, and waste products throughout the body. The **digestive system**—which includes the esophagus, stomach, and intestines—is lined with smooth muscle. It keeps food and waste products moving.

The esophagus has two sets of smooth muscle. One set runs up and down the esophagus, and the other set forms rings around the passage. During a process called peristalsis, these muscles work together to move food down to the stomach. Eventually, the nutrients in the food are absorbed and the waste makes its way to the body's exit. Smooth muscles in an organ called the urinary bladder contract to push liquid waste, or urine, from the body when we go to the bathroom. The same process happens in the colon to

Fast Fact

The tongue is made up of numerous muscles. Unlike most skeletal muscles, the tongue is attached to bone on one end only.

RECEIVING MESSAGES

You don't have to think about moving your smooth muscle cells, but they still need to be told to move somehow. There are different ways smooth muscle cells can receive the message to move. Some react to **hormones** in the blood. Some respond to pacemaker cells that initiate electrical impulses. Single-unit smooth muscle can relay electrical impulses from cell to cell, similar to the way cardiac muscle can. Chemical messengers pass through the boundary between cells. Although all smooth muscle is involuntary, some fibers receive electrical impulses from the brain by way of the **nervous system**.

Different Systems in the Body

respiratory system	helps us breathe
muscular system	helps us move
circulatory system	transports blood
digestive system	processes food and removes waste

respiratory system   muscular system   circulatory system   digestive system push solid waste, called feces, out of the body.

Smooth muscle can also be found in the walls of blood vessels, which are the parts of the body's **circulatory system** that transport blood. Smooth muscle helps keep the blood pumping properly, which keeps us alive.

There are two kinds of smooth muscle. Single-unit smooth muscle is the tightly packed form discussed earlier. Multi-unit smooth muscle, the less common form, is made up of cells that act independently of each other. Each cell connects to a nerve cell so the body can tell it how to act in different situations. An example of multi-unit smooth muscle can be found in the eye. It causes the iris, or colored part of the eye, to grow larger or smaller to let in more or less light through the pupil.

The eye relies on a type of smooth muscle called multi-unit to let in light to see.

Muscles are needed in all activities,
such as long-distance running.

THE BENEFITS OF EXERCISE

Muscles are a big part of daily life. Just about every activity you can think of needs them—even reading and watching television! However, when we work out at the gym, play a sport, or just take a walk, we're using our muscles to make our bodies healthier.

During exercise, the body changes the way it functions to help the muscles work. The lungs take in more oxygen, and the heart rate increases to get more blood to the muscles. This is important because the muscles need oxygen to break down a substance called glucose. We get glucose from the foods we eat.

Creating ATP

Breaking down glucose creates adenosine triphosphate (ATP), which carries the energy that our muscles need to work. The process of combining oxygen with glucose to make ATP is called cellular respiration. When the body doesn't have enough glucose, it breaks down fat to create ATP.

ATP is present in every cell of the body. It fuels

Fast Fact

Our bodies get glucose by breaking down the **carbohydrates** in our food. Foods that are rich in carbohydrates include pasta, rice, and bread.

our muscles, but it also provides the rest of the body with the energy necessary to keep us alive. It fuels the activity inside all the cells of the body. ATP also transports substances across membranes in the body. It helps nutrients get where they need to go.

Like car engines, active muscles burn fuel to create power and movement. Burning ATP creates the waste products carbon dioxide and water. It also releases a lot of heat, which is why we get hot and sweaty during a workout. The muscles contain enough ATP for quick bursts of activity. Then, they need to make more.

During sustained exercise—such as running, swimming, and biking—we breathe deeper and faster, and our heart pumps faster to make sure our muscles have enough oxygen to keep creating ATP. This type of muscle activity is called aerobic exercise. "Aerobic" means "with oxygen." Athletes who require superior **endurance**—such as marathon runners—often participate in daily aerobic workouts as part of their training. However, marathon runners aren't the only people who use aerobic exercises to perform at their best in their chosen

Glucose is found in foods that are high in carbohydrates, such as these.

sport or other physical activity. Cyclists, kickboxers, swimmers, mountain climbers, and dancers do too!

Health for the Heart

Aerobic exercises are often called "cardio." This refers to the cardiovascular system. The cardiovascular system transports oxygen to the muscles and the rest of the body. The main parts of this system are the heart, blood vessels, and blood, which are also collectively called the circulatory system. Regular aerobic exercise strengthens the cardiovascular system and makes it more efficient. It keeps **blood pressure** at a healthy level, burns calories, improves physical endurance, and builds strong muscles.

The circulatory system brings oxygen to all parts of your body, as shown in this illustration.

Anaerobic Exercise

Sometimes, the muscles don't use oxygen to make ATP when doing certain kinds of exercise. This type of muscle activity is called anaerobic exercise. "Anaerobic" means "without oxygen." During anaerobic exercise, the muscles rely on glucose already stored in the cells for energy. This kind of activity also produces lactic acid, which is what causes muscles to feel sore.

Fast Fact

The average heart rate of an endurance runner in a marathon is 160 beats per minute. However, that varies depending on the person's age, height, and speed.

Anaerobic muscle activity does not build endurance. It happens during exercises that last from 30 seconds to 2 minutes.

Lifting weights is an example of an anaerobic activity. When lifting weights, our muscles use quick bursts of energy that don't need to be sustained. This activity creates lactic acid.

At first, lifting weights can lead to muscle fatigue, or tiredness, and then muscle failure. Muscle fibers actually tear during this process. A period of rest is needed for muscle fibers to repair themselves. Your muscles ache while this is happening, but they also grow larger and stronger. The more you lift, the more your body will adapt to the muscle fatigue. Eventually, it will take a lot more weight for you to get tired.

Types of Exercise	
long-distance running	aerobic
sprinting	anaerobic
weight lifting	anaerobic
dancing	aerobic
bowling	anaerobic
tennis	anaerobic
swimming	aerobic

Anaerobic activities rely on quick bursts of energy, such as throwing a bowling ball or sprinting in a race.

STRENGTH TRAINING

Strength training is a form of anaerobic exercise. Most people associate strength training with lifting heavy weights. However, you don't have to lift heavy weights to benefit from strength training. Simpler exercises using only your body are another option for strength training. Using your body weight gives you the same benefits as lifting heavy weights, but it allows you to do exercises wherever you want, at any time of day, rather than going to a gym. No matter which route you choose, the more strength training you do, the easier it will become. Strength training keeps people fit and healthy and helps reduce the risk of injuries during other physical activities.

Fast Fact

Not using muscles enough can result in muscle atrophy, which is a wasting away or loss of muscle tissue.

Strength training can help make your muscles stronger.

Training too hard can result in muscle injury. It's important to balance activity with recovery time and resting.

PROBLEMS WITH MUSCLES

While strengthening your muscles is good for your body, you can also do too much strengthening and cause injuries. Most muscle injuries occur during physical activity or because of overuse. However, they can also occur because of inactivity or an illness.

Common Problems

A strain, or pulled muscle, is a common muscle injury. Normally, muscle fiber is tightly woven. In a strain, the fibers become overstretched or torn. The muscle usually repairs itself within a week. Some strains, however, can last a long time when not properly cared for. A rupture is a more serious strain. This happens when the muscle is completely torn. A small tear can heal on its own. However, a complete muscle tear requires surgery to fix. Some muscle strains and ruptures require **rehabilitation**. A trained professional called a physical therapist can help you recover from a muscle injury.

Physical therapists can show you different exercises to help you come back from a muscle injury.

A cramp can happen suddenly, sometimes in your legs or stomach.

A hematoma is a deep bruise. After a fall or a hard blow to a muscle, blood vessels can break. This can cause swelling and a **blood clot** in the muscle.

Myopathies

Diseases of the muscles are called myopathies. Many are caused by the breakdown of muscle fibers. Depending on the specific illness, symptoms may include pain, weakness, cramps, stiffness, bruising, and swelling. Some myopathies are **hereditary**, while others can happen to anybody. Some muscle disorders are the result of other illnesses. They range from mild to severe.

Some of the most life-threatening myopathies are more than 30 hereditary illnesses called muscular dystrophies (MD). These diseases are marked by weakness and death of skeletal muscles. Some forms affect cardiac muscle.

Diseases like muscular dystrophy affect the muscles, and many don't have cures.

TREATING MUSCLE INJURIES

Being physically fit can help you avoid muscle injuries. However, they can happen to anybody. To avoid muscle injuries, do some light cardio before exercising to get blood flowing to the muscles. Follow the cardio by stretching the muscles you intend to work out.

When caring for a strained muscle, remember the following word: RICE. That stands for rest, ice, compression, and elevation. These are the steps you should follow if you suspect you have a muscle injury. You first rest your body. Then, you put ice on the area of pain. Around the ice you wrap a towel to put pressure on, or compress, the injury. Finally, you prop your injured muscle up on a pillow or similar object at a slightly higher level than the rest of your body. If an injury doesn't improve, you should seek help from a doctor.

Ice is an important part of treating a muscle injury.

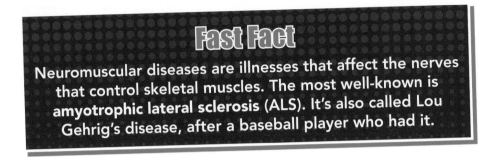

MD can be mild and progress slowly. However, some kinds are severe and fast acting. There's no cure for MD yet, but some people benefit greatly from various forms of treatment.

Myocarditis

Myocarditis is a swelling of the myocardium. Most often, this occurs as a result of a viral infection. Signs of myocarditis include chest pain, abnormal heartbeat, difficulty breathing, fever, swelling in the ankles and feet, and fatigue. This illness is treated with rest and heart medicines. More serious cases may require surgery. If left untreated, myocarditis can result in heart failure, heart attack, **stroke**, and sudden death.

Hungry Muscles

A regular fitness routine is a great way to keep your muscles healthy. However, the harder you work out, the more you need to eat to replace nutrients your muscles use. Healthy carbohydrates—such as whole grains, vegetables, and fruits—provide plenty of glucose for your muscles to turn into ATP fuel. Muscles are made of protein, so it's also important to eat plenty of healthy sources of protein—such as fish, chicken, beans, and nuts. This helps our muscles heal and grow stronger. Be sure to drink plenty of water to replace the fluids you lose while working out and avoid muscle cramps.

To help keep your muscles working properly, it's important to eat healthy food.

The muscular system keeps us moving. By eating right and getting regular exercise, your muscles can be healthy, which means you can be healthy too!

THINK ABOUT IT!

1. How can you keep your muscles healthy?

2. If you were walking a dog, what different muscles would you be using?

3. Stephen Hawking (*shown here*) suffered from ALS. What are other muscular diseases, and how do they affect people?

4. What do you think are the most important muscles in the body?

5. Imagine your favorite sport. Is the activity an example of anaerobic or aerobic exercise?

GLOSSARY

amyotrophic lateral sclerosis: A neuromuscular disease that makes someone unable to move, though the person's brain still functions normally.

blood clot: A hard ball of dried blood that blocks liquid blood from reaching a part of the body.

blood pressure: The force of blood moving through the circulatory system.

carbohydrate: A nutrient in many types of food that the body uses as a source of energy.

circulatory system: The parts of the body that move blood around the body.

complex: Made up of many parts.

cylindrical: Shaped like a cylinder or tube.

digestive system: The parts of the body that process and expel food and drinks we consume.

endurance: The ability to do something for a long time without getting tired.

filament: Something long and thin, like a thread.

hereditary: Passed from parent to child.

hormone: A chemical made in the body that tells another part of the body how to function.

nervous system: The parts of the body that carry messages between the brain and the rest of the body.

nutrient: Something taken in by a plant or animal that helps it grow and stay healthy.

rehabilitation: A process by which a person strengthens injured muscles or areas of the body by performing different exercises.

stroke: A sudden blockage or break of a blood vessel in the brain.

taper: To get smaller toward one end.

FIND OUT MORE

Books

Bennett, Dr. Howard. *The Fantastic Body: What Makes You Tick and How You Get Sick*. Emmaus, PA: Rodale Kids, 2017.

Winston, Robert. *The Skeleton Book*. New York, NY: DK Publishing, 2016.

Websites

Fact Monster: Muscular System
www.factmonster.com/dk/encyclopedia/science/muscular-system
This website breaks down the muscular system with easy explanations.

PBS Science Trek: Muscles
www.pbs.org/video/science-trek-muscles
This online episode of Science Trek explores the muscular system and different muscles of the body.

Strength Training
kidshealth.org/teen/food_fitness/exercise/strength_training.html
Read more about the benefits of strength training, as well as the right way to get started.

INDEX

A
abductor, 9
adductor, 9
aerobic, 18–19, 20
ALS, 26
anaerobic, 19–20, 21
ATP, 17–18, 19, 26
atrophy, 21

B
blood vessels, 7, 15,
    19, 24
bones, 5, 7, 8, 13

C
carbohydrates, 17, 18,
    26
cardiac muscle, 10,
    11–12, 14, 24
cellular respiration, 17
circulatory system, 14,
    15, 19
contraction, 7, 8, 9,
    11–12, 13, 15, 24
cramp, 24, 26

D
digestive system, 13, 14

E
electrical impulses,
    7–8, 11–12, 14
exercise, 6, 17–20,
    21, 25, 27
extensor, 9

F
flexor, 9
food, 6, 17, 18, 26–27

G
glucose, 17, 18, 26

H
heart, 5, 10, 11–12,
    17, 18, 19, 20, 26
hormones, 14

I
injuries, 21, 22,
    23–24, 25
involuntary, 5, 11–13,
    14, 24

L
lactic acid, 19, 20
lungs, 17, 19

M
muscular dystrophies,
    24–26
myocarditis, 26
myocardium, 11, 12, 26

N
nerves, 7, 8, 12, 13, 26
nervous system, 14

P
pacemaker cells, 12, 14
peristalsis, 15
protein, 6, 7, 26

S
skeletal muscle, 5, 7–9,
    11, 12, 13, 24, 26
smooth muscle, 12–15

T
tendons, 5, 8
tetanus, 8
tongue, 13
twitch, 8

W
weight lifting, 6, 20, 21